10866
Robert 2',

10836

Beethown1 #

10836

Blu Swm blad (sxon 1 #

5851

GATHERING SUNLIGHT

*The Poetry
of
Silvia Scheibli
&
Patty Dickson Pieczka*

BITTER OLEANDER
PRESS

The Bitter Oleander Press
4983 Tall Oaks Drive
Fayetteville, New York 13066-9776
USA

www.bitteroleander.com

info@bitteroleander.com

ISBN #: 978-1-7346535-7-1

Library of Congress Control Number: 2022950492

Layout Design by Roderick Martinez

Cover Painting: "Sunflowers" by José Rodeiro. Oil on wood, 30" x 28", 1999
Personal collection of the artist

Manufactured in the United States of America

CONTENTS

Silvia Scheibli
Sky Island Poems

CONTENTS

SKY ISLAND POEMS

Silvia Scheibli

ACKNOWLEDGMENTS

Much gratitude and appreciation to the editors of the following publications, where these poems previously appeared:

Alianza: "On the Malecon in Puerto Vallarta," "Chakira, how will your day begin?" "Song of Bahia de Banderas—Puerto Vallarta, Jalisco, Mexico"

January Review: "Samba in the Sierra Madre," "Duende by the Sea of Cortez, Mexico," "Iguanas and Dogs," "Ode to Iguanas, in Nayarit"

Loch Raven Review: "Mindo, Ecuador," "My Shoes"

Osiris: "Ameca River Jalisco," "Chimborazo," "Song of the Jaguar," "Rim of Fire Volcano," "Alta Mar Siesta," "Jaguar Crossing"

Skidrow Penthouse: "Song of Bahia, Banderas."

An Interview with Silvia Scheibli

BOP: *This book fascinates the reader with the beauty of Mexico's Western state of Nayarit, the Yucatan and then on into the mountains of Ecuador, but it begins with what almost appears to be a mythological character, Chakira. Would you define her for us, what she means to you, and upon whom the first few sequences in this book are based?*

photograph by Roy Rodriguez

Scheibli: I've been looking forward to chatting with you about my latest collection of poems written for the most part in tropical areas of coastal Mexico and Ecuador. I find that the mystical transition between sea, sky and mountains in the tropics is very inspirational. Add to that the ancient voice of Chakira and it is irresistible at times. Chakira is almost family with visionary, intuitive and older-than-dirt qualities that guide me into the past, present and future treating me with her primordial perception that I admire about her. I first met Chakira walking on the beach having just hidden her motorcycle in the dunes. She carried an empty lobster trap on the back for storage. If I hadn't come across this odd parking spot I would have missed her and lost a great chance at a once-in-a-life-time encounter. I am looking forward to visiting with her again next week in Nayarit, Mexico, and hopefully writing more Chakira-inspired poems. Both you and Patty seem to like her too.

BOP: *There are so many wonderous images in these poems, each one teeming with tropical birds, flora, and animals which most of us will never experience. How great is it to not just include them in your poems, but depict the significance of their lives and activities as a way of substantiating the obvious love you have for them?*

Scheibli: As you know I am an avid birder since my days at Tampa University where even red-headed woodpeckers were a common occurrence on campus. Since then my life list has increased to over 500 birds compiled in Europe, Canada, California & southeast Arizona, Kauai, Mexico, Costa Rica and Ecuador. It just seems natural for my feathered friends to flutter in and out of my poems with me. I'd like to say a few words about the title, Sky Island Poems. Sky Islands are known for their incredible biodiversity and natural beauty arising to more than 6000 ft from the desert floor. This is where jaguars meet bears, where bromeliads grow in the arms of oak trees. Natt N. Dodge referred to the Chiricahua Mountains in southeastern Arizona as "mountain islands in a desert sea." The term "Sky Island" was later made popular by nature writer Weldon Heald. The more I explored these magical, rugged and remote lands the more fascinated I became; so much so that I joined the Sky Island Alliance in Tucson that is protecting and restoring the diversity of lands in the Sky Island region.

BOP: *Would you say all of these poems were written while in each particular locale or were you simply capturing fragments as rapidly as possible for eventually writing them into future poems?*

Scheibli: Writing each poem is a little bit different. For example, in Ecuador I wrote complete poems on the bus from Quito to Babahoyo to Guayaquil and Mindo, where I stayed over-night in a treehouse. In Nayarit and Playa del Carmen I wrote poems in a cabana on the beach listening to the rhythm of the surf. If there was time I would complete them and edit a bit later. Images would spark and I would grab my cell notepad and start writing. I could compare this process to photography in that capturing an image at a precise moment one needs the camera handy. Then one can process the image at a later time. Add or delete shadow & color, crop & zoom, but the composition is in place. For me writing poems is very similar to this photographic process.

BOP: *Filtered throughout this book is the deep compassion you show for those you either saw or actually met and this kind of interaction occurred whether you were in Playa Ayala, along the Rio Cuale, in Guayaquil, or gazing up at the snow atop Chimborazo in Ecuador. In fact, this whole book is a compassionate text of life. How, as a background for these poems, does it seem to come to you so naturally?*

Scheibli: Writing hasn't always come to me naturally. I have kept an open mind and set a course to appreciate my surroundings wherever I am. I raise orchids, a hobby that requires a lot of attention and patience but is ultimately rewarding. I watch birds, which is almost a sport in that it does require certain physical stamina and again takes a lot of attention. Then I am a photographer that needs focus. All of these activities help me pay attention to my environment where I attempt to SEE the world around me. Writing poetry is all about how one sees where one is or where one would like to be. I've given a whole bunch of examples of how I go about writing a poem, but left out the basic one. READING. Reading the great poems like Samuel Taylor Coleridge's "Kubla Khan," or "A Vision in a Dream," is a wonderful way to be inspired or meet one's exclusive muse.

SKY ISLAND POEMS

"As a man is, so he sees.
As the eye is formed, such are its powers."

— William Blake

PART ONE

Duende Poems

Chakira, tell me once again

Oh, tell me how the moon
opened your eyes and showed you
a change in consciousness

How you wished that every coyote
should have a black-tipped tail

How the oriole's hood
was dark until you changed it
to reflect indigo sunlight

Nothing appears natural now—
Now you dream the raven in silver.

How do you dream only in silver, Chakira?

My friend, Chakira, gave me her chisme

"Listen," she said.

Pelicans glide on wings
as straight as paddle-boards.

Aero-dynamic frigates ascend
immense, azure skies.

Supplicant, boat-tailed grackles
seek verdant, queen palms.

Caffeinated kiskadees
exclaim an immanent sunrise.

You need to visit Nayarit—
opaline goblet of barefaced dreams—
more often.

Chakira, how will your day begin?

Will it begin with the yellow-winged screech of the caciques?
Or the iguanas lazing in the palms?

Maybe the black breast of a frigate chasing a phantom sail in the surf?

Will it be the white-gold plume of the boat-billed heron
in mangrove forests?

Or will it begin with the Citreoline Trogon
on a wire in Playa Ayala?

Will it be with the group of dolphins
spinning near the fishing boat?

Will it be with the jaguar, bronze eyelids squinting in mangroves?

Or the great-tailed grackle on the palapa?
Or the muddy sash of the alligator?
Or the empty lobster trap on the motorcycle?

Or the stingray in the fisherman's net, set free again?
Or the disgruntled cartel fighters jailed now?
Or the loco taxi drivers?

Or fire opals the colors of lipstick?
Or the sunken, delirious, red eyes of bromeliads in swamp banks?
Or the polished, long necks of royal palms elegant in green?

Or the brandied-gold of sorghum fields at sunset?
Or the serene brush strokes on the turquoise bowls set for dinner?

Nuevo Vallarta is a bracelet one never takes off.

Song of Bahia de Banderas — *Puerto Vallarta, Jalisco, Mexico*

A blanket of light
undulates between Jupiter and the moon
over Bahia De Banderas.

Like a giant hammock
the Sierra Madre are suspended
above the Puerto Vallarta malecon
where souls of Santa Guadalupe
kneel on beach sand and negotiate their sins
with lustrous prayers of magnificent frigate birds,
carnivores & magpie jays
unaware of the span of salty wind
emanating forgiveness in this Aztec penumbra.

Obscure yet enflamed
in the foothills of imagination —
heavy glances
registered in the names of Tin Tan
or his cousins at Mismaloya
or the arches
of 'The Night of The Iguana,'
forever idolized
in the archives of Hollywood.

The real black iguanas
rest heavy-lidded eyelids
on shifting voices in the flea market
where multi-beaded jaguars
and rounded-cheeked carvings
caress transparent trout-like fish
that spawn on even more
transparent sand in the Rio Cuale.

On the bridge to old town
intrinsic malcontents
sculpt handprints on painted masks
that sprout from palapa walls
borrowing spirits of the dead
barely surviving on crutches or even pedestals
depending on calculated adventures
in the midst of opulent, tequila embraces.

On the Malecon in Puerto Vallarta

Boys smile like Formula-One drivers
race copper seahorses
in coffee paintings

White-linen girls wipe bleached
counters with dreams
crossing their hearts

Zebra butterflies dance along with jasmine

Magnificent frigate birds
glide like whispers
into my blood — their aerodynamic, angular silhouettes
carve phantom sails
on motorcycle mornings

Azul eyelids
piña colada lips
Aztec cheekbones
salty hands
promise you everything
but give you a
Citreoline Trogon
sitting on a wire in Playa Ayala

Duende by the Sea of Cortez

I am surrounded
by sun-baked palm fronds
& lime green, iguana willows
on a golden river bank with bronze flower spikes.

I hear orange-fronted parakeets
with azure eyelids like islands in the sea
screech near fire opal bromeliads.

By the Sea of Cortez
where Mayans & Aztecs wrote their visions
on black granite boulders in feathered fields
with pythons tangled in branches above pictographs
I sense the sacred language
delineating decades of struggles
to work corn & bean fields
to free the earth & wear it like a terra-cotta poncho
across heart & shoulders

Wearing the land like music
on hands, hips & legs
they treated the dirt like a dance
sharing days with barking dogs in the dust of the road
& greeted each morning like tropical kingbirds
with an ancient screech at sunrise

Asleep in the cloud forest at night
death ignited their dreams
of opalescent orchids whose beaks like scarlet macaws
awoke the sleeper inside —
the one full of pride in plain dirt
reborn & newly etched each morning

Samba in the Sierra Madre

Samba sounds
spill over opalescent sand
rising to jaguar sky islands
like empty hands
sleepy with last night's dream

Combing the moon's gold-speckled hair
mountains in an ultra violet jacket with foggy collar
drift in a thermal haze
& shift the afternoon's music
from the boardwalk to the bay
where snowy egrets & frigate birds
open the sleeves of bamboo palms
buttoned down by a breeze

Ameca River, Jalisco

Sitting on a wire

by a dirt road

a blue-black grassquit

flashed prismatic

in early light

Focusing on nothing in particular

except dried grasses

shifting with the breeze

and gentle cows

herded to pasture

Ode to Iguanas in Nayarit

Parakeet-green & coconut-clawed

        iguanas bask in dream-filled palms

     taste melon sunlight

           & tout spectacular tails

as their heavy Mayan eyelids

     stay motionless

         eternal

          divine

Under the Palapa

There she is

living dreams

she dreamt

while sick

Watching black-masked kiskadees,

green, long-tailed iguaneros,

brown pelicans & snowy egrets

thread the needle

on el Bahia Banderas,

Nayarit

Cancun Triptych

Road to Xcaret

Full moon
filled to the brim with her ocean
does not fall & fish do not drown

Yellow-faced caracaras
two by two
drag the coruscating wind like sultry towels
over straw roofs capped by chromatic rain clouds

The Yucatan peninsula
with a twist of rice & black beans
reveals the many faces of quetzal,
the feathered serpent,
for whom the jungle pulsates &
heaves three rivers of mangroves
like glistening veils across the sun

For centuries
sultanate green eyes of jaguars
battled darkness and reinvented the dawn
each morning

Iguanas and Dogs

Pre-Columbian astronomers & priests
gathered in civic plazas for ceremonies—
addressed entire populations.

Carried limestone for building materials
wore a sacred cast
of wind god, water god, and rain god.

Human hearts were fed to symbols on stucco walls
& colorful paintings of jaguars —
the venerated beings
of their time.

Mayans still prosper.
600,000 descendants live & speak Mayan today.

Indigenous cultures
with brick & mortar structures
for socializing in plazas
made of native limestone &
Spanish architecture
stand today.

Plazas as
literal & political centers—
principal streets &
churches with
four universal paths—
of heart, mind, action & spirit.

My question is — are iguanas and dogs still sacred?

Alta Mar Siesta

Tired mangroves
close liquid, azul eyelids

Green iguanas sleep — hardly breathing

The swamp yields
malachite shoulders of pelicans
& leans
into the amber hour

Just as the sun sets sail
like a Mayan, feathered serpent
chasing catamaran clouds

Jaguar Crossing

At the jaguar crossing

on the main road to Cancun

we imagine an opalescent shadow

moving in mangroves

where the serpentine heat

flicks its lusty tail

The yellow street sign

with the jaguar drawing

stirs the hieroglyphic deity

wrestling night terrors

reviving the sun

& melting our illusions

each morning

Song of the Jaguar

Lime-feathered jaguar
      conveys a message with
neon syllables
  to my bones of eagles & serpents
      in tones of fire

No power equals his — not the ocean
     beneath the surface of Jupiter,
  nor the exquisite, bromeliad jungle
heat

   Only monsoon rains
are devoted to soothe
   my quetzal-blistered tongue.

Cabo Still Life

Bronze goddess

      in oceanic dress —

Arms a straw basket filled with

      tangerine light

ablaze with chatter of spiny, cactus wrens

Opens

      snowy, balcony curtains

            like vermilion ocotillos

      after a storm

Song of the Orange-fronted Parakeet

Screeching bromeliads

    in forked branches of primavera trees

emphasize

       dreams

The velvet crown of

       emerald primordial voices in my sleep

 glistens like opals

      beneath the yellow eye ring

  of you

      my feathered serpent

Life is a Blue Jaguar

Chakira writes that life in Nayarit is a blue jaguar,
a tanzanite blue, whose mystery is revealed
by a solitary golden-cheeked bird that keeps hiding.

She said that she can't depend
on the Laughing Falcon to point the way to eternity
and that I must visit soon or both of us would be lost.

So, I wrote back saying
how much I admire her work as an Huichol artist —
when Covid is done I'll book a flight
and we'll search for the golden-cheeked one together.

Apurate!

Nayarit

In Nayarit,
Chakira submerged
the crimson glow of her eyes with muffled tears.

The pandemic strangled her and
unfolded a craving for freedom.

Like two swallows,
we washed pebbles in mud &
whispered for dawn
to reveal her silver sleeves.

In Nayarit,
Chakira instilled
orchids with yearning &
me with terrestrial secrets.

Grita on Madero and Aguacate

Humidity is a luna moth
crawling down my neck.

If only we had one of those yellow street umbrellas
hanging in the exhibit on Madero
across from the pharmacy by the taco truck
whose driver sped to the scene
of a woman hit while crossing the street.

If only the monsoon would show up
instead of drinking tequila
for nights on end
wallowing in uncertainty.

If only gas were cheaper again
so we wouldn't be walking
with the sun's ashes racing in our veins.

If only the taxis had A/C.

If only I had worn crocks.

If only we had booked a water taxi
and I hadn't heard the woman
dying on the cobblestones —
one shoe twisted under the wheel.

Hymn of the Guitarron

—for Cesar

The liquid evening
    ignites the heart of the quetzal

brings me the entire night sky —

all the stars with their
    emerald feathers & the
blood moon —

to graze
    on your bronze darkness
        roosting with your name
on my syllabic shoulders

Hymn to Seawater

The face of your underlying
    darkness has a chiseled form

that tries to merge
    with the light breaking in my voice —

    like a ring I no longer remove —

I awake with your hands calling my name

    blueish-white curtains as if

submerged in seawater

        define our touch

Humidity

Humidity like a blanket of salt,
steam and sand assaulted my skin.

Chakira waved for me to join her under the palapa.

She was selling cocos & pineapples as hot as ice.

Staring at the horizon
a strong rip-tide &
a speed boat's rooster tail
blurred our vision.

Ameca River

Chakira's motorcycle
with lobster trap handles
leaned against drift wood
piled on a sand bank.

She proposed we meet
where oyster catchers snooze,
where the cool current of the Ameca
flows into the warm bay.

Waves from the river
curled against the bay's surf,
embracing smooth, black lava pebbles.

Brine foamed through our fingers.

El Estero

At dawn Chakira and I watched
darkness flow like glass
past red legs of stilts.

I was hoping the sun would stay behind mountains,
for robust fishermen to stand still by their nets,
for sleep-walking, gray iguanas
to transform into green branches.

For humidity to wade upstream
slow as clouds.

PART TWO

Ecuador Poems

"Art is a way to encompass love."
— Guayasamin

For My Friends in Ecuador

Land of hospitality!
Land of the Andes & Amazonas!

With lush corn fields & many-colored roses,
ruby bromeliads & golden bananaquits,
scent of cocoa & coffee plantations,
where even fence posts bloom again,
the open spirit of your condors &
the force of your green rivers
created your grace, your gentleness
and your kindness.

Abrazos!
I will always remember you!

Cotopaxi

—for my good friend & translator, Gina Lopez

Cenizas! You welcomed us
with open arms &
covered us
with your ashen kisses.

With grit on our tongues
we dug deep
into your marbled skies,
somehow blackening our tears
with your welcome.

Like your trees,
roads & horses,
we needed a new skin —
skin scrubbed clean of conventions
that hold no water.

So we could feel anew
your agave flowering,
with doors, windows & steps
opening the blood on blood
of the jaguar woman
waiting inside
all of us.

Chimborazo

—for Jose Marzumillaga

Snow-covered Chimborazo,
like the snow-white collar of the condor
hovers on the backs of sheep & huts,
tractors & cows,
clotheslines & chimneys.

The musical flight of the condor
glides over the faces of dogs,
fields of dried corn & goats
that answer only to the wind
and Pacha Mama.

Mindo, Ecuador

Mindo's cloud forest
snakes like an emerald alpaca scarf
tossed over trees &
wrapped in a lapis knot
by the long-waisted river
cascading over tropical cliffs.

Like one continuous call to prayer
the steaming foliage
calls up uncalculating rain drops
on the slick, darkened earth &
fern rooftops splashed
with black & yellow butterflies.

Yet within this cacophonous
jubilation of fauna
one can feel the thick fur
of solitude bind our every breath,
creep behind our eyelids
& fall asleep.

Echos on the Road to Babahoyo

Geese & dozens of jungle chickens
scratch endlessly on hillsides
of banana trees.

Escaped sugar cane & emerald mist
engulf abandoned houses.

Bromeliads perch on telephone wires
like mourning doves.

With partially opened wings
black vultures cast a shadow
over yellow hibiscus.

Delicate roof ferns
volcanic rock & golden bamboo
fade into midnight
with our cafe
con alma socialista.

Rim of Fire Volcano

Ash & rocks
lava rings among weeds
on mango & saffron church walls
on lilac painted houses

In cumbia plazas
history is recorded with ceramics,
penas of agave azul
Mayan designs of feathered serpents
ancestors speak mathematical syllables
with water still flowing
in irrigated corn fields
two thousand years
later

My Shoes

—for Neruda's Socks

In the blazing Ecuadorian sun
step by step
humidity curls my hair &
begs for any sign of a breeze.

My yellow shoes,
canvass - no match for
cobblestones in Guayaquil —
walk without complaint.

They make no comment
at the sight of street dogs
asleep in the same spot
each day by bloodshot day.

They don't linger at store windows
with chocolate pavlovas
or cafe con leche at intimate
tables for two.

They don't compare prices
of chicken or pulled pork burritos
with rice, pinto or black beans
at los carritos.

They don't give a rip
about what kind of ice-cold cervezas
guys had for lunch
with their grilled cuy.

Stepping lightly in Iguana Park —
sudden long tongues & tails
scurrying through tall grass —
avoided at all costs! No problem!
They don't even care
about being stuck in airplane mode
on the flight to Quito
sitting in the middle seat.

A tad jealous
my canvas shoes cringe
when a fancy, new Panama hat
is tipped with a smile.

Beyond
These Poems
There Be Dragons

Patty Dickson Pieczka

ACKNOWLEDGMENTS

Grateful acknowledgment to the editors who published these poems, or earlier versions of these poems, in the following publications:

Ann Arbor Review: "Dancing on Democracy's Grave," "Highwayman's Moon," "Roots from the Deepest Soil"

The Bitter Oleander: "A Broken Road," Echo," "I Thought You Were a Desert," "Last Day of Vacation," "Opening the Dawn," "Weaving the Night"

Forge: "Under an Electron Microscope"

January Review: "At Horseshoe Lake," "Election Year," "Refugees"

Osiris: "Crystal Visions," "Following this Ancient Map," "Search for the Center," "Stormscape," "The Language of Shells," "Wroclaw, 1945"

Scarlet Leaf Review: "Misplaced"

Screech Owl: "Beyond this Place There Be Dragons"

Shot Glass Review: "She Died in Autumn"

An Interview with Patty Dickson Pieczka

BOP: *Before reading this selection of your poetry, it would be helpful to understand who these dragons might be that lay in wait beyond these poems. What do they represent for you?*

photograph by Johnny Pieczka

Pieczka: First, Silvia and I would like to thank you for conducting this interview for our collaborative collection. The original intention of the title, of course, was inspired by ancient maps indicating a ship might fall off the edge of the world or encounter dragons if it went beyond known and conventionally recognized land boundaries. I like the idea that each poem might take the reader beyond accepted or approved limits of thought, that words might open new worlds and concepts not before considered, a process of moving past the ordinary that can often be a frightening or exhilarating experience, symbolized by the sighting of a dragon, its huge teeth and green scales flashing in the light of its fire, tail thrashing the ocean into a spray of water, churning up a cloud of steam and smoke, a new dimension contained in each drop's colorful prism. A third meaning (and personal joke) is that due to physical limitations, I now use an audio device for writing called the Dragon, so behind and beyond each poem I've written, there truly is a Dragon.

BOP: *As your previous books have shown, your poems are written as though in a dream sequence where anything can happen and often does. The only difference is that you are in control of this sequence, can determine its images, and bring it to life. From where does this ability originate?*

Pieczka: Writing is such an interesting and unusual process. It can start with a word, a phrase, a visual image or even a color. Then it begins to expand, and as it does, it's as though something or someone else begins to take over, a sort of channeling, as if falling into another dimension, a dream-like place. Though I'm still aware of writing, this inspirational voice introduces ideas I'd never imagined. Sometimes, hours can pass. There's a finished poem in front of me, and it feels as though I'd only been working a few minutes. I've spoken to other writers about this, and many of them experience the same kind of thing. My dad used to call it "the big hand in the sky." I didn't know what he meant until it happened to me.

BOP: *Four of the poems in this book are what, for lack of a better term, might be called circular or linked poems. Each of the four poems is comprised of four parts. Each part begins with the last line from the previous part and the very last line of the final part is identical to the very first line of the poem. How did you happen to write these pieces as they appear?*

Pieczka: I never seem to know when a "linked" poem is on my horizon. They always begin as a single short poem and often stay in that form, but sometimes the last line of a poem lingers in my mind for quite a while and eventually morphs into a new direction for the next part of the poem. Once I realize it's turning into a chained poem, I make sure each section ends with an interesting line that could create a new tangent. As it gets going, each new part seems to quickly follow previous section, and the poem develops a circular path of its own. I love writing this sort of poem. It's so interesting to see where the words take themselves.

BOP: *The mixture of the natural world with your emotional state at the time each poem was written makes for a unique sensitivity where one does not outweigh the other. How do you continue to manage the same balance achieved in* Beyond These Poems There Be Dragons?

Pieczka: Nature has always been important to my sanity and spirituality and is often woven throughout my poetry. As you know, my husband and I live near the Shawnee Forest, which makes an appearance in much of my work. We go there to recharge our emotional batteries, connecting with our original roots and source of being. These poems were written at different times and in different states of circumstance and inspiration, so what you're noticing is probably this sense of the natural I try to bring home with me and carry in my mind: bird calls, splashes and wing-flutters, wind rippling dark streams shaded by vines, sounds from the beginning of time often mistaken for silence in the woods.

Beyond
These Poems
There Be Dragons

Nature is the art of God.

— Dante Alighieri

Following This Ancient Map

Time inhales, pulling the earth.
Buildings vanish. Stone houses
sprout from fields
near the village monastery.

Pavement crumbles into cobblestones,
falling away to this donkey-cart path
that leads us to sea
under dog-eared, yellowing skies.

We board a tall ship and sail away,
far from the present with its
dust-strewn dreams,
its thorn-toothed truth,

off to a place of sweet papayas,
second chances, the scent of mint
near the edge of our map,
singed by dragons' breath.

Beyond This Place There Be Dragons

Drifting on an ocean's
silk and shells, sea-foam
lacing pearls along the shore,

I follow a dream back
to its home in the dark,
unlace the night
to find forgotten things:

half-vanished thoughts, time
curled within my root,
words melted by a long-ago sun.

I drift to the ceiling
to watch you sleep.
Your dream breaks
over shoal-bound rocks,

shaking loose a school
of silver fears
and familiar strangers

who sail angel-winged ships,
read the 16 points
of a wind rose to navigate
through the moon's veil

and ghosts of fog
to the farthest edge
of the subconscious.

The Language of Shells

Sibilant song,
Whisper of storm and sea,
wind scraping across mud flats

that once held water,
wind flowing through me,
through this phantom lake,

its wounded kayaks and wedding rings,
skeletons of better days
when we'd splash, waist-deep in August

or curl into afternoon's warm shell,
listen as willow fronds stirred the water
and daydreams drifted in paper boats

until sunset painted the snow geese
into a flaming island of feathers
that flew toward the moon.

Weaving the Night

Hulking trees follow me
to the lake.

They lean over to remove
their green hoods, wave
black lace veils

in dances that stir the sky.
Clouds open to reveal
the night's crystalline heart.

Sadness and fear burn away
on shooting stars.
Dreams wash up on shore.

In the morning,
the ground disappears.
I step on air,

surprised to find
it holds my weight.

Crystal Visions

i.

Some days words refuse to levitate
or be pulled from a hat.

They beach themselves
in sand, sun-drunk and lazy,

will not reach deeper
than their own shadows

to detect a thin crack growing
along a porcelain vase

or the faint scent of sorrow
vining the rose lattice.

Some days words cannot open
their third eye to read

the names of the missing afloat
inside this beveled crystal.

ii.

Inside this beveled crystal
            I see my mouth full of night,
hands grasping at nothing, hear

my heartbeat's syncopated arrhythmia
            of loss. How will I stand,
supported by shadows, knee-deep

in memories and hopes so thin
            their ribs show through
their web-sheer gowns?

The future is best left to itself,
            mumbling secrets to its long fingers
from inside cages of roots

away from the leafless light. Will
            I drink from this moon-stained river,
shape a new day from mud?

iii.

Shape a new day from mud.
Let worries fall like white petals
in a snow garden,

while memories flap through the sky
like startled birds, shrinking and fading
until the horizon inhales them.

Sculpt this morning from gold, jade,
the wings of egrets.
Plant yellow wildflowers

in the darkest forest
while remaining
hours walk the sundial.

iv.

Hours walk the sundial,
sleepwalk through light.

Days keep melting around corners
as time coos from the mourning

dove's beak and slips like silk
through rustling leaves.

I want to write a new ending,
change these visions that haunt

my mind, heavy as stone, but
some days words refuse to levitate.

From the Throat of Sunrise

I wake on the roof to find
my dream has lost its voice
and forgotten its prayer.
Its colors sift to the street below.

The day has a bite taken out of it.
Everyone is hungry,
chewing off bitter hours.

I try to patch the hole
with sweet cherries, melons,
the earth's tears.

How does one atone for desiring
baked apples, blackberry wine,
a squeeze of pineapple between the lips
during this season of loss?

As salvation slips behind a cloud,
morning hides beneath my tongue.
The sun melts.

Under an Electron Microscope

Nucleotides twist
into a ladder of tiny pearls.
A twirl of DNA ropes
into sedge and steam.

A man steps down
from its dangling,
bare feet imprinting clay.

He carves out his life
with a musk-oxen horn,
carries hammerstone
and a bear-tooth awl.

His woman buried near
a scorch of caribou,
he migrates through
the woodwind valley,

carries his son
down the sacred melt
through dogtooth violets
and gooseberry deer paths.

The silver stream has learned
her voice, her laugh, curves
its arms to touch him.

As trees whelm the earth with
darkness, he breathes a fire
from flint and rock, throws
his heart into the flame.

A charred stone in his chest,
he searches for God's face
in wavers of smoke and spark.

At this end of the microscope,
I wear his hungry eyes.

I Thought You Were a Desert

I never saw the toucans
flying
through your heart

nor the orchid
that could grow
from your tongue.

I only noticed
how fire plants flamed
in your eyes
when you spoke,

veiling me in ash.

Our conversations skimmed
over water
like a curl of leaf.

Any deeper current
pulled us under.

Opening the Dawn

i.

Morning falls from my eyelashes –
    these jungle-thick woods,

how sunlight lanterns through leaves
    spilling gold into your hands,

kissing the vine-shaded stream
    before wind takes its first breath.

My dream slips among the trees
    to mingle with whispers,

its colors blending with larkspur,
    the city reduced to reflected flame.

ii.

The city reduced to reflected flame,
    in its light I see the breath kneed
from its throat, hungry fires.

The day folds in on itself,
    trees bowing to the ground.
Clouds slog hip-deep through the marsh.

A rift cuts through these hills;
    the grass shivers to one side,
unwilling to cross.

How could I, with these hands of twigs,
    this wind-torn heart, pull cobwebs
from the world's eyes,

make it see its own humanity, see
    how morning's wings could open
to let its origami swan take flight?

iii.

Let its origami swan take flight.
We could float
above plague-ridden crowds,

above fiery rooftops
where prayers drift, cough smoke
from their lungs.

Souls rise, some ready to ascend
into this red-stained sky, others
try to return to their bones.

This high up, the mind takes over.
When sounds cannot become words,
voices lose their shapes.

iv.

Voices lose their shapes
              as food lines snake through town
with fear-tinted fangs.

The city's ribs protrude
              like steel girders
over this crust of dried grass.

A thin crack colors the horizon
              in the direction
of the woods, paints us wild ginger,

paints us cherry sweet, sends us
              back to our moon-candled tent before
morning falls.

Last Day of Vacation

Morning ripens, peels
its lemon-candled dawn
to puffs of fragile lace.
Light fills my hands,
dripping sunrise:

the scent of yellow,
of plantains, parrots
squawking colors to the sky,
the echo of shoes clicking wood
on the mangrove bridge.

My heart grows a rind
to protect this spark.
Tomorrow's problems stand
shivering in a crooked line;
their breath brittles
into tiny frosts of teeth.

A Broken Road

Taste of snails, of salt,
of remorse; opals of blood
necklace the moon.

Unbraid the night song
smoking through my hair.
Empty the lake from my eyes,
the sap from my bones.

I will give these things
to walk backward, to send
the sun from west to east,
to float a leaf upstream

and make the clear path visible
through knives of sunlight,
each sweet polkberry dripping
its own poisonous word.

I reach into the past
with hands of dust.

Midnight Visit

i.

Star-blown and dream-torn,
I come to you, carry
the moon on my shoulder, hoping

you'll unstitch your sleep
and dream me into
your mind, to that place where fear

dissolves on the tongue
and flies on
breath-light wings of white moths,

where nightmares catch flame,
clatter
into piles of bone and fangs,

claws strung
into bracelets,
that place where your warm skin

melts ice from my thoughts until
they sprout
white wildflowers.

ii.

White wildflowers,
        soft beneath my feet,
spread their blanket
        over our black lawn.

Hydrangeas ghost their way
        up the trellis.
Blossoms teach me
        how to unfurl,

to become vapor, invisible,
        to look through skin
and read hearts,
        to distinguish those filled

with starlight or rippling silk
        from the ones who
press knives to
        the throat of sunrise.

iii.

The throat of sunrise
opens, crimson and hungry,
ready to swallow me into the day.

I see inside my eyelids
this recurring fall.
Will you catch me

this time like an angel
with outstretched arms?
Or will I again hear

sounds of bone-crack
and time-shatter,
this limping clock

ticking fractured moments,
the slip-crumble of rock as
air rushes past me?

iv.

Air rushes past me,
      deep-sleeping breath

as your dream escapes,
      steaming from the pillow:

silken pieces of color,
      unfamiliar memories.

I touch your warm arm, curl
      into your flight

past the ceiling, through rough-grained
      roof shingles, to that place

between primrose evenings
      and cello-sweet light,

far from harsh edges
      and flame-shooting fear,

away from all that is
      star-blown and dream-torn.

Roots from the Deepest Soil

A bean vine curls up my ankle
like the illegible scrawl
of a dream that spilled
during the darkest ink of night.

Behind clusters of emerald broccoli
and rhubarb fans, acerbic,
tomato-red faces seem to know
secrets buried in my mind,

the indigo smoldering
just beyond reach.
Brussels sprouts whisper,
peeking from their layered leaves.

I yank at lush greens,
pull up a beet, muddy truth
clinging to its root.
Its musky-sweet, earth-blackened
magenta drips my regret.

She Died in Autumn

—In memory of Patty Taylor

Final moments fall to her fingers,
where they perch like paper birds.

In her chemo-brushed voice,
she manages a joke, but her thoughts

are for her daughter
wandering a motherless world.

This hornbeam she planted
outside her window

roots into deep earth,
searching for strength.

She becomes its leaves—russet,
gold, crimson—coloring themselves

in their finest grace when they
sense death approaching.

As the clock wanders
its senseless circle,
my father asks who I am.

My name becomes
the wrong shape,
a broken song,
its swollen syllables
thick on my tongue.

Letters drop from my mouth
to my lap, surprising
as fallen teeth.

My voice is a goat's bleat.
My voice is carved from ash.
My voice summons locusts and moths.

The years collide
and slip into
my father's shirt pocket.

He looks at me
through confused eyes,
the frayed air
creased and yellowed
as an old photograph.

Half Moon

Wading through shadows,
sensing the faint slosh of memory
as darkness slaps against my mind
like the side of a creaking boat,

I listen for sleeping butterflies,
the voices of stars, a grass blade
seeding its new poem to the breeze.

I want to know how cicadas learn
to sing their pain, how
an owl's call tunnels

through deep woods and circles back,
bearing dreams of light
to the dark edges of leaves,

how I am carried through loopholes
of time by sounds seeking
a soft place to land
among grief's silver footprints.

Search for the Center

My mind shifts
like a sack of sand,

pulled by moon,
tides, evil tales.

Where is the compass,
the level, the protractor
that finds middle ground?

Dreams leak out
my window,
spark into the sky.

An unfinished poem
catches fire in the corner,
ashes brushing my shadow.

Election Year

begins as it always does,
like a mosquito, its tiny buzz
assaulting the ear, the agility
of acrobatic tongues:

words broken and glued back together,
words scooped empty, hollow
and ringing, words cracked open
and drained of their juice.

Breezes brewed of shattered sounds
melt sun into gold that slips
into pockets, melt hatred
into sweet dark wine.

Reason peels like birch bark,
sifts to the wind, as voices
of the lost and seeking hiss
and steam through spirals of mist.

Echo

I pulled thunder from his voice
and put it in a jar, hoped
the glow of its lightning
could somehow lead my way.

Its glare blinded me.
Glass shattered,
painted red rivulets
across my hands.

I hid his thunder behind a curtain
of night, filled that slack-jawed space
between failed efforts
and snake-bitten goals,

that place between wall and rafter
where prayers get wedged
on their journey upward.
Loud rumbling kept me awake.

I buried it—dropped it
like a string of black pearls
clattering against the wood
of its tiny coffin.

Mud-crusted skeletons
sent their broken-tongued ghosts
to my dreams to complain
of noise.

Dancing on Democracy's Grave

Dance the pulse of this burning hour.
Let crackling music writhe through your bones.

Dance the color of the sky on fire,
of justice crumbling,
mouths full of echoes.

Hunger growls
beneath flame-shot clouds cracking
into blood-rubies.

A shard falls,
carves the day in half.

Dance in singed clothes
on this ragged ridge of earth.

Refugees

We live on the border
between swallowed songs
and wings.

Moon slides down our backs,
but darkness holds our hands,
guiding us blindly.

Home has become this goat path,
narrow and winding as a snake
in the brush.

We walk along its slippery back,
careful and quiet,
trying not to wake it.

We mix the night's pain
with pigments of ground plum petals,
malachite and berries

to paint ourselves
into this landscape.
Salvation is hidden

somewhere among black jacarandas.
Our silken hope slips
through these dark branches.

WROCLAW, 1945

— In memory of Pola and Kazik

Surprised the day's heart still beats
when sunlight lies prone in the street,
and wounded trees, so thin and wasted,
fan the scent of death lodged in his nose,
thunder rumbling his mind.

What could be restored from nothing?
He wades through the rubble of lives:
a broken helmet, machine-gun casings,
shredded dress fabric. Unnamed fears
wind among flowerpot shards, a table leg,

dreams crushed under crumbled buildings.
A hand grenade pin flashes from the ruins.
He imagines how it would look,
polished and hammered flat as the sun,
a wedding ring to sparkle from Pola's finger.

December in the Era of Madness

Winter flashes his mirrors,
peers into them and cannot
find himself,

sees Spring wandering lost
down the street, her green hat
vining a gold-leafed ginkgo,

roses blushing
the old wooden fence
where mosquitoes whine.

The scarecrow, wearing
sunglasses and a beach towel,
watches geese fly north.

Winter's angry skull leers
down from the clouds.
His detached body,

this huge and whirling funnel,
spins toward us
in the night.

Stormscape

When the moon blows out its candle,
night asks for mercy

from this landscape of limbs
and dishes and flying souls.

Courage seeks its own redemption
but stumbles into darkness,
cut and wounded.

Our house's skeleton clatters
across the field and slumps
to its knees.

I shout your name and wind
gusts from my throat.

Clenching your shadow
between my teeth,

the weathervane's horse
galloping through my hair,

I wade through night's black water
toward morning shores of purple phlox.

Only in Shadows

Beyond flame-sky
and dream-smoke,
beyond thundering thorn-sparks
and the sharp tongues
of falling knives

where nothing exists
but smooth sweet cherimoya
and kiwano melon.
Sun-baked fantasies
create substance:

a blind sorcerer
leaves his silver magic
where light opens
spaces between leaves.
Morning unfurls
its ostrich feathers.

Morning unfurls its ostrich feathers
          and mimosa leaves, fringing the world

beyond my eyelashes until tornadoes exist
          only in shadows pulled by dreams.

Sometimes the mind can bench press
          the body, read the day's thoughts

before the sun wakes, see what hides
around corners or creeps up from behind.

Sometimes the mind opens as though
          swallowing the universe.

iii.

Swallowing the universe,
infinity swirls inside me—
        solar systems compose my heart,
stars sparkling through my veins.

        Purple brume clouds my ribs,
carries me to the mouth of time.
        Dimensions intersect.
Crows flap, perch over letters

        burned into wooden crosses.
Walking along this horizon where life
        and death touch, my feet tick
ten years forward with each step,

        leaving no footprints in the salt.
My body loses substance, bones hollow.
        Dark forests engulf me,
green vines me, sap-filled.

iv.

Green vines me, sap-filled,
through flashing diamonds of sun.

Earth has regained its rhythm,
echoing music of heaven.

Thrust and pull of new life
forces my third eye open.

All nature enters me.
I am dove, magnolia, mountain lion,

read thoughts, know the feel
of a butterfly's flight, see into minds.

Time trembles, shakes
leaves from my quaking limbs.

I struggle to remain in this place
beyond flame-sky and dream-smoke.

Highwayman's Moon

Tiny wings shiver
through my veins,
anisette, foxglove.

Ghost of a dream
drifts through the window
on its scent of witch-grass
and meteors, smokes you
across my mind.

Morning yawns the curtains
into my room. A gumbo-spiced
breeze pulls you
to this door.

The Morning After

If you'll fan the morning's blues
into peacock feathers,
I'll melt night's bullet casings
into wind chimes and teach them
to sing in the breeze.

If you'll be a palm tree
moved by wind's exotic secrets,
I'll wear the ocean's jewels,
sun-sparkled and glittering,
and scatter them at your roots.

If you'll turn night's drive-by
into a dance across sand,
I'll be the surf's voice,
the shape of time forgotten,
music silking between leaves.

At Horseshoe Lake

I pull sunlight from your hair
to make our shadows pour
into the cypress swamp,
where rivulets spill back
to the time we met.

Tupelo leaves brush the colors
left by secrets barely whispered—
words beyond flight
and dream, strung to
neither root nor bone,
words tumbling in shapes
never recognized before.

We unbutton the hours
until day and night
meet briefly at the horizon;
they kiss, still making
each other blush
after so many years.

ABOUT THE POETS

Silvia Scheibli has served as judge for the 2017 Bitter Oleander Press Library of Poetry Book Award. In 2015 she was invited to Ecuador in a cultural exchange of poets between the United States and Ecuador touring and reciting in the Amazonas as well as in Quito, Babahoyo and Guayaquil with Alan Britt and Steve Barfield. Besides publishing eight books of poems including, *The Moon Rises in the Rattlesnake's Mouth* (Bitter Oleander Press), *Under The Loquat Tree* (2002, Vida Publishing), and *Parabola Dreams* co-authored with Alan Britt (2013, Bitter Oleander Press), she is the editor and publisher of *Cypress Review* and CypressBooks since 1980.

Graduate of the University of Tampa, Tampa, Florida, in the late '60's she studied with Duane Locke, founder of the Immanentist Movement in poetry. Along with Alan Britt, Paul B. Roth, José Rodeiro and Steve Barfield, the Immanentist poets still thrive in the United States, Europe and South America and everywhere where a visionary approach focuses on primordial nature similar to the surrealism and Deep Image poetry of Federico Garcia Lorca, Pablo Neruda, Karl Krolow and others. Immanentist poems are embedded with passion and spontaneity and loved for their universal Duende qualities.

Scheibli has published in *Cholla Needles, Osiris, Bitter Oleander, Ann Arbor Review, Black Moon, The Midwest Quarterly, The January Review* and *The Raw Seed Review* among others. She is an enthusiastic photographer and birder living near the borderlands in southeast Arizona where jaguars, bobcats, coatimundi, white-tailed deer and javelina move freely.

Patty Dickson Pieczka's third book of poetry, *Beyond the Moon's White Claw* won the David Martinson Meadowhawk Award from Red Dragonfly Press. Her second collection of poetry, *Painting the Egret's Echo*, won the Library of Poetry Book Award for 2012 from the Bitter Oleander Press. She was the featured poet in their Spring 2014 issue and was invited to serve as book contest Judge in 2019. Other awards include the Maria W. Faust Sonnet Contest in the Best Sonnet category, the ISPS poetry contest for 2012 (first place in the free verse category), Frances Locke Memorial Poetry Award for 2010, and nominations for an Illinois Arts Council Award and three Pushcart Prizes. Other books are *Lacing Through Time* (Bellowing Ark Press, 2011), and a chapbook, *Word Paintings*, (Snark Publishing, 2002).

Patty graduated from the Creative Writing Program at Southern Illinois University. Writing contributions have appeared in many journals, including *Bluestem, Blue Unicorn, The Cape Rock, Crab Orchard Review, Eureka Literary Magazine, Green Hills Literary Lantern, Red Rock Review, Sierra Nevada Review, Versedaily.org, Willow Review.* Her first novel, *Finding the Raven*, was released in June 2016 by Ravenswood Publishing. Visit her website at http://www.pattywrites.net/

THE BITTER OLEANDER PRESS
Library of Poetry

TRANSLATION SERIES

Torn Apart by Joyce Mansour
(France)

—translated by Serge Gavronsky

Children of the Quadrilateral by Benjamin Péret
(France)

—translated by Jane Barnard
& Albert Frank Moritz

Edible Amazonia by Nicomedes Suárez-Araúz
(Bolivia)

—translated by Steven Ford Brown

A Cage of Transparent Words by Alberto Blanco
(Mexico)

—a bilingual edition with multiple translators

Afterglow by Alberto Blanco
(Mexico)

—translated by Jennifer Rathbun

Of Flies and Monkeys by Jacques Dupin
(France)

—translated by John Taylor

1001 Winters by Kristiina Ehin
(Estonia)

—translated by Ilmar Lehtpere

Tobacco Dogs by Ana Minga
(Ecuador)

—translated by Alexis Levitin

Sheds by José-Flore Tappy *
(Switzerland)

—translated by John Taylor

Puppets in the Wind by Karl Krolow
(Germany)

—translated by Stuart Friebert

Movement Through the End by Philippe Rahmy
(Switzerland)

—translated by Rosemary Lloyd

Ripened Wheat: Selected Poems of Hai Zi **
(China)

—translated by Ye Chun

Confetti-Ash: Selected Poems of Salvador Novo
(Mexico)

—translated by Anthony Seidman
& David Shook

Territory of Dawn: Selected Poems of Eunice Odio
(Costa Rica)

—translated by Keith Ekiss, Sonia P. Ticas
& Mauricio Espinoza

The Hunchbacks' Bus by Nora Iuga ***
(Romania)

—translated by Adam J. Sorkin
& Diana Manole

To Each Unfolding Leaf: Selected Poems (1976-2015) by Pierre Voélin
(Switzerland)

—translated by John Taylor

Shatter the Bell in My Ear by Christine Lavant
(Austria)

—translated by David Chorlton

The Little Book of Passage by Franca Mancinelli
(Italy)

—translated by John Taylor

Forty-One Objects by Carsten René Nielsen
(Denmark)

—translated by David Keplinger

At an Hour's Sleep from Here by Franca Mancinelli
(Italy)

—translated by John Taylor

Outside by André du Bouchet
(France)

—translated by Eric Fishman & Hoyt Rogers

I wander around gathering up my garden for the night
by Marie Lundquist
(Sweden)

—translated by Kristina Andersson Bicher

Consecration of the Wolves by Salgado Maranhão
(Brazil)

—translated by Alexis Levitin

Tango Below a Narrow Ceiling by Riad Saleh Hussein
(Syria)

—translated by Saleh Razzouk with Philip Terman

The Butterfly Cemetery by Franca Mancinelli
(Italy)

—translated by John Taylor

* Finalist for National Translation Award from American Literary Translators Association (ALTA)—2015

** Finalist for Lucien Stryk Asian Translation Award from American Literary Translators Association (ALTA)—2016

*** Long-Listed for National Translation Award from American Literary Translators Association (ALTA)—2017

ORIGINAL POETRY SERIES

The Moon Rises in the Rattlesnake's Mouth by Silvia Scheibli

On Carbon-Dating Hunger by Anthony Seidman

Where Thirsts Intersect by Anthony Seidman

Festival of Stone by Steve Barfield

Infinite Days by Alan Britt

Vermilion by Alan Britt

Teaching Bones to Fly by Christine Boyka Kluge

Stirring the Mirror by Christine Boyka Kluge

Travel Over Water by Ye Chun

Gold Carp Jack Fruit Mirrors by George Kalamaras

Van Gogh in Poems by Carol Dine

Giving Way by Shawn Fawson **

If Night is Falling by John Taylor

The First Decade: 1968-1978 by Duane Locke

Empire in the Shade of a Grass Blade by Rob Cook

* *Painting the Egret's Echo* by Patty Dickson Pieczka 2012

Parabola Dreams by Alan Britt & Silvia Scheibli

Child Sings in the Womb by Patrick Lawler

* *The Cave* by Tom Holmes 2013

Light from a Small Brown Bird by Rich Ives

* *The Sky's Dustbin* by Katherine Sánchez Espano 2014

* *All the Beautiful Dead* by Christien Gholson 2015

* *Call Me When You Get to Rosie's* by Austin LaGrone 2016

Wondering the Alphabet by Roderick Martinez ***

Kissing the Bee by Lara Gularte

* *Night Farming in Bosnia* by Ray Keifetz 2017

Remembrance of Water / Twenty-Five Trees by John Taylor

The Stella Poems by Duane Locke

* *Ancient Maps & a Tarot Pack* by Serena Fusek 2018

Not All Saints by Sean Thomas Dougherty 2019

* *Blue Swan, Black Swan: The Trakl Diaries* by Stephanie Dickinson 2020

Weightless Earth by Paul B. Roth

Tracing the Distance by Andrea Moorhead 2021

Come Closer by Laurie Blauner 2022

* Winner of The Bitter Oleander Press Library of Poetry Award (BOPLOPA)
** Utah Book Award Winner (2012)
*** Typography, Graphic Design & Poetry

All back issues and single copies of *The Bitter Oleander* are available for $15.00
For more information, contact us at info@bitteroleander.com
Visit us on Facebook or www.bitteroleander.com